Essay Examples: The Easy Way!
Contains examples of 15 different five-paragraph mini-essays

Peggy M. Houghton, Ph.D.
Timothy J. Houghton, Ph.D.
Edited by Pamela A. Presnal

Education is one of the best investments you will ever
make…and our books maximize that investment!
Houghton & Houghton

Section	**Page Number**
Introduction	3
Types of Essays	3
Analytical	4
Argumentative	5
Cause	6
Comparison and Contrast	7
Critical Analysis	7
Definition – Specific	8
Definition - Subjective	9
Descriptive	10
Effect	11
Expository	12
Illustration/Exemplification	13
Narration	14
Persuasive	15
Process - Information	16
Process – Direction	17
Conclusion	17

Introduction

Many people struggle with writing essays. The process of generating a topic, organizing thoughts, and composing the document in a way that makes sense and flows logically can be overwhelming.

There are a lot of books written that tell you how to construct an essay. They use definitions and rules to form the building blocks of the process. This is great for some people…but it does not work well for others. Some people need examples to visualize what they are going to write, and this book is for those individuals.

The structure of the book is straight forward and simple. Fifteen different types of essays are identified, defined, exemplified (using a mini-essay), and explained. The types of essays include the following:

Analytical
Argumentative
Cause
Comparison and Contrast
Critical Analysis
Definition – Specific
Definition - Subjective
Descriptive
Effect
Expository
Illustration/exemplification
Narration
Persuasive
Process - Information
Process – Direction

The section for each type of essay includes the following:

- A definition of the essay being examined.
- An example of the essay being examined (using a mini-essay).
- A *Notice How* section that identifies the introduction, body, and conclusion of the essay being examined.

If you are a person who learns by example, then this book is for you.

Types of Essays

Let's start with a simple rule. Regardless of the type of essay being written, the basic structure is the same:

- The introduction presents an idea.

- The body supports the idea.
- The conclusion summarizes what was written and offers additional insight.

This structure might seem rudimentary, but it is adequate. You can use it for all essays…regardless of their length. For this book, a five paragraph essay is exemplified (using a mini-essay) because that is typically the most commonly utilized.

Remember to always properly cite your sources. You don't want to write a good essay and receive a failing grade for plagiarism.

Now let's move into the various types of essays.

Analytical

Essays emphasizing *analytical* thinking examine something. The goal is to convince people that the examination is valid.

Example of a mini-essay emphasizing analytical thinking

Chicago is a large American city located in the state of Illinois. It is a frequent destination for people all over the world with multiple daily stops made by airplanes and trains. It is one of the best cities in the United States because it has so much to offer.

One of the main attractions of Chicago is the downtown nightlife. Many of the bars and restaurants are world class, and they are often open until the early morning hours. There is rarely a time when people can't find something to do, and public transportation makes it easy to get anywhere.

Chicago also is a major center for theater. Improvisational comedy originated there, and many actors honed their crafts on local stages. Broadway employs thousands of people and provides millions of dollars in revenue for the Windy City.

In terms of architecture, Chicago much to offer. Many great modern day architects have designed buildings downtown because the 1871 Great Chicago Fire destroyed most of the original dwellings. This makes Chicago unique because the buildings are famous for their originality, rather than their age.

Chicago is truly a great city. The night life, theater, and architecture make it an excellent place to live or vacation. If you need more proof, then just ask the millions of visitors and residents.

Notice How:

- **Introduction** - The first paragraph gives a broad overview of Chicago.
- **Body** – The second, third, and fourth paragraphs analyze positive aspects of the city

---

from a cultural perspective.

- **Conclusion** – The fifth paragraph summarizes the culture and notes that is a great place to travel or reside.

Argumentative

Essays emphasizing an *argumentative* viewpoint establish a position. The goal is to sway the reader into agreeing with the writer.

Example of a mini-essay emphasizing an argumentative view

Paying college athletes has recently become a hot topic of discussion. Some people believe college sports should remain an amateur competition where sportsmanship is at the forefront and players are not monetarily compensated. Others argue that it is time to pay players because the college sports world is vastly different since the rules were established many years ago. I believe the times have changed, and so should athlete compensation.

First and foremost, college athletes bring in huge revenue for their schools. Millions of dollars are made from advertisers, fans, students, and alumni. The schools profit while the players do the work. This is simply not fair.

Another unfair aspect is the fact that most college athletes will not play professionally. This might be the only opportunity they have to get paid for their skills. The current financial situation is a win-lose. The universities win, and the athletes lose.

If college athletes did get paid, the only people who would lose are the ones who should. Payments from dishonest boosters, recruiters, and agents would be eliminated. Right now, these individuals have a great opportunity to illegally funnel money to players in exchange for wins or future favors. If the athletes were paid by the schools, money from unscrupulous people would no longer be needed.

Some sports fans argue that college sports should promote amateur competition only, and the athletes should not be compensated. While this viewpoint has some validity, it is not fair. The players bring in huge revenue for their schools and might never have the opportunity to make money professionally. Unscrupulous individuals also profit illegally when the players do not get paid. It is hard to determine exactly how much money athletes should make, but there needs to be some type of financial reward system in place. Maybe a payment cap is the answer.

Notice How:

- **Introduction** - The first paragraph shows both sides of the argument for athletes getting paid, and then it takes a position.

- **Body** – The second, third, and fourth paragraphs present arguments for student athletes being monetarily compensated.
- **Conclusion** – The fifth paragraph summarizes why athletes should make money and offers an idea for a payment structure.

Cause

Essays emphasizing *cause* start with the effect and then determine the cause.   In other words, what made the event happen?

Example of a mini-essay emphasizing cause

Farm animals in the United States are dying at an early age. Chickens are not living long enough to lay eggs, and hogs and cattle are perishing before they are old enough to breed and reproduce.

Early death rates in farm animals are the result of several different factors. Air pollution from cities is finding its way into rural communities. Factories in urban areas are churning out smoke that is damaging to the environment for miles around. Animals need clean air for healthy living, and it is not always available.

Contaminated river water is also an issue. Tainted water from industrial areas flows into rural communities where it is used by farmers for their livestock. Despite environmental rules and regulations, some companies still use rivers for the discharge of waste.

Lastly, there is overcrowding of animals being raised on farms. Gone are the days when animals roamed freely on open ranges. Tough economic times have forced farmers to make more money using less space, and this acts as a catalyst for spreading disease.

American farmers are losing their livestock at a young age due to the industrial waste, land shortages, and the economy. The United States government needs to create stricter laws for pollution in order to curb this devastation. The government also needs to provide financial aid to the farmers to prevent them from going out of business. The time for action is now, or farming might just become another industry that is outsourced to foreign countries.

Notice How:

- **Introduction** - The first paragraph discusses the effect of farm animals dying young.
- **Body** – The second, third, and fourth paragraphs identify the causes of these deaths.
- **Conclusion** – The fifth paragraph summarizes causes of premature farm animal deaths and offers suggestions for preventing this in the future.

Comparison and Contrast

Essays emphasizing *comparison and contrast* start by comparing similarities and end by contrasting differences. In other words, comparing shows how things are alike, and contrasting shows how things differ.

Example of a mini-essay emphasizing comparison and contrast

Police officers and security guards are employed throughout the United States. They work at events, patrol public and private areas, and represent authority by the uniforms they wear and the vehicles they drive.

Their jobs are similar in some ways. For example, they both work to protect the rights of citizens and make sure people adhere to rules and regulations. In this respect, they make sure that the law is upheld.

They also both prevent people from violating established procedures. For example, they might get involved if someone cuts in front of other people who are waiting in a line. Cutting in line might not be a crime, but it is does violate customary protocols.

While police and security guards possess some similar job responsibilities, they also differ in certain ways. For example, police officers have greater authority in larger areas. They might oversee an entire city, where a security guard might only oversee a single department store. Police officers also have the right to arrest people within their jurisdiction, while security officers can only detain them until a police officer arrives.

In summary, police officers and security guards are similar because they uphold laws and established procedures. However, their range of responsibility and authority also makes them different. It might be a good idea to have them working side by side at the same functions because they share common goals, but work within different jurisdictions.

Notice How:

- **Introduction** - The first paragraph discusses police officers and security guards.
- **Body** – The second and third paragraphs identify the similarities of police officers and security guards, while the fourth paragraph identifies their differences.
- **Conclusion** – The fifth paragraph summarizes the similarities and differences of police officers and security guards and suggests that they work together.

Critical Analysis

Essays emphasizing *critical analysis* offer evaluations of text. Generally, they take on an argumentative form based on the author's opinion.

The Ramones wrote many short and powerful songs based on a driving chainsaw guitar that kept their fans bopping and hopping. Their clever lyrics concentrate on simple and funny aspects of life. They make light of people's everyday activities by bringing them to the forefront of their music.

One song, however, stands out as being different from the rest. "Danny Says" does not contain Johnny Ramone's signature guitar riff. It is a ballad with a sensitive and somber tone. It is about being in love with someone and missing them while out on the road touring.

There are some humorous aspects of this song, like when Joey Ramone sings about how it is too cold to go surfing in Idaho because it is 20 degrees below zero, but the overall vibe is a serious one. When you are in love with someone and have to leave that person, nothing seems to fill the void.

The most interesting part of the song focuses on the group members making promotional appearances and conducting interviews. One might think that fame is appealing, but the lyrics tell how Joey can only think about reuniting on the following day with the one he loves.

"Danny Says" is a solemn ballad. It has some funny lines, but the song speaks of the pain experienced by being away from the one you love. Even rock star status does not prevent you wanting to be with that person. This is summed up well in the line, "It ain't Christmas if there ain't no snow." In other words, it is no holiday being on the road without the love of your life.

Notice How:

- **Introduction** - The first paragraph discusses typical Ramone's songs.
- **Body** – The second, third, and fourth paragraphs critique "Danny Says."
- **Conclusion** – The fifth paragraph summarizes the song and expands upon the meaning.

Definition

Essays emphasizing *definition* explain the meaning of a word, which aids in understanding unfamiliar concepts and terms. This pattern is very useful for the sciences since terminology can be very *specific* to the discipline. However, it is also used for other disciplines, such as political science and humanities, in a more *subjective* manner.

Listeria monocytogenes – scientific definition

Listeria monocytogenes is a genus of the species Listeria. It is found in many different environments and has been identified by the CDC (2004) as a serious health threat to humans.

This pathogenic, gram-positive, rod-shaped, flagellated bacterium does not form spores. It is a stable organism that can grow in the presence or absence of oxygen and is capable of reproducing within the host.

Because Listeria monocytogenes is a hardy organism, it is a major food safety concern in certain types of processed meat and cheese products. It primarily affects pregnant women and people with weakened immune systems, and it can be fatal.

Listeria related health issues can largely be avoided by cooking, handling, and storing food properly. Most commercial food manufacturers have programs in place that address these processing procedures in order to prevent any type of outbreak.

Listeria is a pathogenic organism that can grow and reproduce with or without oxygen, and this makes it a concern for certain processed meat and cheese items. Listeria related illness can be avoided by properly handling these foods, but it might be a good idea for pregnant women and those with weak immune systems to avoid eating them.

Notice How:

- **Introduction** - The first paragraph describes Listeria monocytogenes.
- **Body** – The second, third, and fourth paragraphs identify specific properties and effects of Listeria monocytogenes.
- **Conclusion** – The fifth paragraph summarizes Listeria monocytogenes, and offers advice for those who might be affected by it.

Example of a mini-essay emphasizing definition (subjective)

Conservative – political definition

United States conservatives are people who share similar principles. They believe in maintaining traditional American values and empowering people for problem resolution.

Part of empowering people means limiting the government's role. Essentially, conservatives think the government should exist to provide freedom for people to embark upon their own endeavors.

One way to uphold people's freedom is to provide a strong national defense. Conservatives want the military to be strong, so principles can be defended when outside adversaries attempt to change them.

While conservatives value overall freedom, they frown upon individual freedom guaranteed by government protection of civil liberties. They view this as forced action that benefits few people and harms the majority.

Conservative people typically respect traditional institutions, prefer limited government, desire a strong military, and dislike abrupt change to established order. They stand firm in their beliefs and have helped make America the great country that it is today.

Notice How:

- **Introduction** - The first paragraph defines conservatives.
- **Body** – The second, third, and fourth paragraphs identify the beliefs of conservatives.
- **Conclusion** – The fifth paragraph summarizes conservative thinking, and notes the positive effect of their actions.

Descriptive

Essays emphasizing a *descriptive* view describe a person, place, thing, or situation. In other words, they enable the reader to visualize and form an impression of the topic of discussion.

Example of a mini-essay emphasizing a descriptive view

Europe has always interested me. Each country has its own unique character, and sightseeing is wonderful throughout the continent. The people are also welcoming, culturally astute, and willing to answer questions from curious tourists.

My favorite city in Europe is Amsterdam. The country of Holland is known for beautiful windmills and countryside, and Amsterdam complements this well as a bustling, vibrant city. The people there speak excellent English and are incredibly friendly. It's simple to navigate on foot through the lively Red Light District and surrounding small shops, and public transportation makes it easy to get to any remote area of the city.

Amsterdam also has a lot of history. One of the most famous places is Anne Frank's house. Anne was a young Jewish girl in hiding who kept a now famous diary during the World War II German occupation. Her life as a prisoner in her own home is detailed as people tour her house. Actual artifacts used by her family, such as furniture and utensils, are displayed as portions of her diary are read by the guide. I honestly felt like I was living during the occupation as I walked through this historical landmark.

The most interesting thing about Amsterdam is the fact that it is built on a peat and bog. Canals continually drain water in order to keep the land from becoming swamped. Since the peat and bog are too soft to support buildings, many structures are built on long wooden piles that are driven into the ground until they reach a stable layer of sand beneath. I am truly in awe of this this architectural wonder.

My fascination with Amsterdam is endless. It has culture, history, gracious people, and is literally built on water. When I go there, I feel respected and welcome. Because of this, I will return.

Notice How:

- **Introduction** - The first paragraph tells why Europe has always interested me.
- **Body** – The second, third, and fourth paragraphs describe the city of Amsterdam.
- **Conclusion** – The fifth paragraph summarizes my description and notes that I will go back.

Effect

Essays emphasizing *effect* start with the cause and then investigate the effect. In other words, what happened because of the event?

Example of a mini-essay emphasizing effect

Andrew Oldham should have left earlier for work this morning because he was tardy. His boss, Amanda Jones, was unforgiving since this is the third time he was late this month. She told him that he must arrive at work on time for the rest of this month or he will be terminated from his position.

Andrew's tardiness has resulted in many problems at his company. Other employees have complained because they have had to fill in for him during his absence. The company is growing at a rapid pace, and people barely have time to do their own jobs. Finding someone to fill in for Andrew makes a difficult situation even worse.

On the days Andrew arrives late, he is sleepy and disorganized. He has trouble performing his job responsibilities, and this makes things more difficult for everyone else. Andrew's coworkers rely on him to properly complete his portion of a project before they begin to work on it, and he makes many mistakes when he is tired.

The worst part about Andrew's mistakes is that he gets defensive when he is confronted. He makes up excuses and tries to blame other people for his errors. This creates a hostile work environment that most people would rather not work in.

Andrew's tardiness results in issues within his company. When he is late, his coworker's workloads are increased, and they are forced to wait on completing projects. Andrew also makes a lot of mistakes on the days he is tardy. He blames others for his errors, and this creates a very stressful environment. Andrew must take his job more seriously. He needs to get to bed earlier so he will not be tired the next day. He also needs to leave for work earlier in the morning to assure he will be on time.

Notice How:

- **Introduction** - The first paragraph discusses tardiness as the cause of Andrew's job being threatened.
- **Body** – The second, third, and fourth paragraphs identify the effect of Andrew's tardiness on his coworkers.
- **Conclusion** – The fifth paragraph summarizes the effects of Andrew's tardiness and offers suggestions for preventing this in the future.

Expository

Essays emphasizing an *expository* view divulge important information about something. This helps people make informed decisions about the topic.

Example of a mini-essay emphasizing an expository view

People in the United States are choosing not to smoke. This is not surprising based on the wealth of information available on the negative effects of smoking. The Center for Disease Control (2008) found that less than 20 percent of the population smokes, which is the lowest percentage since the 1960s. More encouraging is the fact that there is no indication that this downward trend is going to change.

Research clearly indicates people associate lung cancer with smoking (Martin, 2005). Aside from medical study findings, the obvious correlation comes from the inhalation of smoke directly into the lungs. The resulting closed capsule environment is perfect for carcinogens to destroy human health. Watching a loved one suffer or die from lung cancer leaves a lasting impression on many people, and smoking is often a big part of that picture.

Lung cancer is not the only cancer that results from smoking. The Surgeon General's report (2004) found harmful linkages with the stomach, cervix, pancreas, and kidney. These diseases are treatable in some instances, but in other cases they are fatal. This deadly concern caused the government to invest considerable time and effort into publicly attacking smoking, and people decided to listen.

The government and other public interest groups have gradually changed the American perception of smoking (Sauls, 2011). It has been many years since the Marlboro man made his last television appearance, and movie actors and actresses appear out of place with a cigarette dangling from their mouths. Quite simply, tobacco is taboo in many people's minds; and the end result is a reduction in the smoking population.

Fewer and fewer Americans are smoking. Medical studies have convinced them that tobacco products result in adverse health issues, and cancer is the main culprit. Public campaigns mounted against smoking have been effective, causing people to refrain from lighting up during their drive to work, after dinner, or during a good conversation. This is great because decreased smoking equates to a national decline in disease and death. Quite simply, people are getting it…before it gets them!

Notice How:

- **Introduction** - The first paragraph exposes the fact that Americans are choosing not to smoke.
- **Body** – The second and third paragraphs describe the negative effects of smoking. The fourth paragraph explains why public opinion about smoking has changed.
- **Conclusion** – The fifth paragraph summarizes why Americans are not choosing to smoke and tells why this is good.

Illustration/Exemplification

Essays emphasizing *illustration/exemplification* illustrate or exemplify the main idea. This can be done with one example or a few examples, and a story or a quotation might be used. The key is to clarify the main idea.

Example of a mini-essay emphasizing illustration/exemplification

Rhonda Sienkiewicz wants to be a chef at a premier hotel in New York City. She graduated from college with a degree in culinary arts, and she is now pursuing her goal of working at a fine establishment in the "Big Apple."

One of Rhonda's culinary arts professors, Christopher Conklin, was a big influence on her. Christopher told her, "The way to a person's heart is through his or her stomach, so become the best chef you can to everyone."

Mr. Conklin also taught Rhonda that people have different tastes, so she learned to cook a large variety of foods. She did this in part by watching the Food Network on cable television. Her favorite episodes focused on the diversity of New York restaurants.

Tom Kinney, host of Food Network's *Big Cities with Big Appetites,* has said, "You can get any food you want in New York…all you have to do is turn the corner." Rhonda is well aware of this and realizes she will have to do the best job possible to keep people from leaving her establishment in search of better food.

Rhonda Sienkiewicz has a goal to become a chef at a fine hotel in New York city. Her college professor and the Food Network have instilled in her the importance of learning to properly cook a variety of foods in order to achieve that goal. She is ready to move forward with her career, and she appears to be headed in the right direction.

Notice How:

- **Introduction** - The first paragraph describes Rhonda Sienkiewicz's chef aspirations.
- **Body** – The second, third, and fourth paragraphs support how she will be able to achieve her goal.
- **Conclusion** – The fifth paragraph summarizes her ambition and training, and ends by stating that she is ready for success.

Narration

Essays emphasizing *narration* use a related story. Stories capture people's attention, and narration uses details for enticement. Typically, the narration starts at the beginning of the essay and leads the reader to the analysis or argument.

Example of a mini-essay emphasizing narration

When I was a little boy, I used to look at older kids and wish I was one of them. I thought they were very knowledgeable, and they were always doing something exciting. In short, I wanted to be their age so I could live like they were living.

Older kids could go concerts and parties without their parents. They were not on a set schedule and could come and go as they pleased. My friends and I needed to get permission to go anywhere. If permission was granted for a specific activity, we had to have an adult accompany us, and there was usually a pre-established start and end time.

Older kids also talked about things that I found interesting. They discussed driving cars, going out to eat with friends, water skiing behind fast boats, and attending college football games. These were things that I wanted to do, but I was too young.

I eventually reached the age of the kids I admired. I got to do the same things that they did. I went places and attended events with my friends, and we had a lot of fun. Overall, this was a beneficial life lesson for me because I learned that good things come if you wait.

The thought of getting older always excited me when I was young. Older kids were mentally smart and physically strong. They had the freedom to go places without adults, and they talked about things that were attractive to me. When I finally reached the age of those kids, I enjoyed the same things. I realized the wait was worth it!

Notice How:

- **Introduction** - The first paragraph begins the story of how I wanted to be older.

- **Body** – The second and third paragraphs use details to show why I wanted to be like the older kids. The fourth paragraph tells what happened when I reached their age, and then then makes the argument that good things are worth the wait.
- **Conclusion** – The fifth paragraph summarizes my reasons for wanting to be older and notes my eventual realization.

Persuasive

Essays emphasizing a *persuasive* viewpoint convince people to perceive something in a particular way. The goal is to persuade the reader.

Example of a mini-essay emphasizing a persuasive viewpoint

Many people choose not to go to college. Their education ends at high school graduation because they do not have the time, desire, money, or support to continue on. The purpose of this writing is it to show you the importance of obtaining a college education.

The first reason you should go to school is to enhance your ability to learn. Regardless of your career path, you will need to learn, and college teaches you how to do that.

The second reason for going to college is employment opportunity. College graduates typically have a broader range of careers to choose from then those without degrees. They also do not have to start at the bottom (sweeping floors or cleaning bathrooms) when they are hired, and the initial wage is often a livable one.

The last and most important reason you need to go to college is income potential. While many business owners are successful without college degrees, they are the exception. College graduates have consistently out earned non-graduates over the past 50 years. Master Degrees and Doctoral Degrees make even more money over the course of their career (AIE.org).

In summary, college graduates know how to learn, have more job options, and a have better earning potential than those without degrees. Time has repeatedly shown that a college education pays off. The time for action is now, so pick your school and get started.

Notice How:

- **Introduction** - The first paragraph discusses the fact that some people do not go to college, and then begins to discuss the importance of higher education.
- **Body** – The second, third, and fourth paragraphs present arguments for going to college.
- **Conclusion** – The fifth paragraph summarizes why people should obtain a college degree and encourages them to start now.

Process

Essays emphasizing *process* explain (1) how something works by *providing information* or (2) the procedure of doing something by *providing direction*. In other words, they help people understand the steps or protocol involved.

Example of a mini-essay emphasizing process (providing information)

Incandescent and fluorescent light bulbs are used by essentially everyone in the world. People use them at home, work, and during leisurely activities. While most individuals know how to turn on a light and replace the bulb, few know how they actually work.

Incandescent lights use electrical current to heat a tungsten wire filament that glows and produces the light we see. Tungsten burns up when exposed to oxygen, so the filament is sealed in a glass bulb that is evacuated or filled with inert gas. The seal voids all oxygen, thereby preventing destruction of the wire.

Halogen lamps are also incandescent lamps that use electrical current. These bulbs, however, contain a small amount of halogen that allows them to operate at elevated temperatures. The life of a halogen bulb is extended using a chemical reaction that works to redeposit evaporated vapor back on the filament.

Fluorescent lights are not incandescent bulbs. They use a glass tube filled with argon gas and mercury. Electrical current passes through the gas, picks up energy, and radiates that energy as heat and ultraviolet light. The ultraviolet light then reacts with a coating on the inside of the glass tube causing it to glow.

Incandescent and fluorescent lights both operate on electrical current. Incandescent lights work using a tungsten filament that glows. Halogen lights function by using halogen that allows them to operate at high temperatures. Fluorescent lights operate using argon gas and mercury. All three lights are good in different situations, and sometimes they work together to provide light for people all over the world.

Notice How:

- **Introduction** - The first paragraph discusses the fact that most people do not know how incandescent and fluorescent light bulbs work.
- **Body** – The second paragraph provides information about how incandescent lights work, the third paragraph provides information about how halogen lights work, and the fourth paragraph provides information about how fluorescent lights work.
- **Conclusion** – The fifth paragraph summarizes how each bulb works and notes that they can work independently or together.

Example of a mini-essay emphasizing process (providing direction)

Passports are required for all United States citizens traveling to foreign countries. If you are going to apply for your first passport, then you need to follow a basic three-step procedure.

First, you need to acquire proof of identification and proof of citizenship. The best document for proof of identification is a valid driver's license. The best document for proof of citizenship is a birth certificate.

Second, you need to submit your proof of identification, proof of citizenship, and application in person to a designated passport location. Most local post offices are designated passport locations, but you should call or check on line to be certain.

Third, make sure you apply well before the date you plan to travel. A passport can take up to three months to process, depending on the number of people applying, and you cannot enter a foreign country without one.

In summary, passports are a required for United States citizens travelling to foreign countries. In order to obtain an initial passport, you need to properly identify yourself and apply in person to a designated location. Plan to do this at least three months in advance of your travel date to avoid unanticipated delays. Visiting foreign countries can be a wonderful experience, but without a passport, you will not be able to do so.

Notice How:

- **Introduction** - The first paragraph tells you about a three-step procedure for applying for a passport.
- **Body** – The second paragraph specifies the documents you need. The third paragraph informs you where to apply. The fourth paragraph warns you to apply well in advance of your travel date.
- **Conclusion** – The fifth paragraph summarizes the application procedure and notes the consequences of failing to do so.

Conclusion

This book contains multiple examples (mini-essays) of commonly used essays. It is beneficial because now you can focus on content, rather than structure, in order to succeed in developing and writing essays.

The great part about this book is you can always refer back to it when needed. Just apply the mini-essay example to your topic and expand upon it as desired. It truly is *the easy way* for essay writing.

Words for College Papers and Presentations: The Easy Way!

Peggy M. Houghton, Ph.D.
Timothy J. Houghton, Ph.D.

Education is one of the best investments you will ever
make…and our books maximize that investment!
Houghton & Houghton

A

1. Abecedarian – person learning the alphabet
2. Abderian – given to idiotic laughter
3. Abdicate- relinquish, resign
4. Aberration- deviation, abnormality, delirium
5. Abet- assist, sanction
6. Abeyance- cessation, doldrums, hiatus
7. Abhorrent- loathsome, offensive
8. Abject- degrading, contemptible
9. Accede- agree, assent
10. Accord- agreement, adapt, grant
11. Accubation – reclining while eating or drinking
12. Acquiesce- assent, comply
13. Acumen- insight
14. Adjourn- defer, prorogate
15. Ad hoc – improvised, impromptu
16. Adoxography – writing in praise of unimportant or trivial subjects
17. Affiance- undertake to marry, betroth
18. Affidavit- sworn statement, deposition
19. Aghast- horrified
20. Agog- ardent, appetent
21. Agraffe – a hook or clasp
22. Ague- shivering, fever
23. Akimbo- with angles
24. Albatross – constant worrisome burden
25. Alienate- estrange
26. Ambiguous- equivocal, vague, cryptic
27. Ambuscades- ambush
28. Amelioration- editing
29. Amid- among
30. Amiss- wrong, astray, incorrectly
31. Anachronistic- archaism, prolepsis, antiquated
32. Anathema- detestation, horror, odium
33. Anomalous- abnormal
34. Anopisthography – writing only on one side of a piece of paper, tablet, leaf, etc.
35. Antechamber- waiting room
36. Anxious- apprehensive, concerned, eager
37. Aped- primate, copy
38. Aperture- hole, fissure, orifice
39. Aphrodisiac- carnal, erotic
40. Apocryphal- of doubtful authenticity, spurious, fake
41. Apostate- deserter of one's faith, dissident
42. Apprehension- anxiety, understanding, seizure, idea
43. Apprised- informed

44. Appurtenances- accouterments, gear
45. Arabesque- needlework
46. Ardor- zeal, mettle, lust
47. Arrayed- decorated, festooned
48. Ascend- rise, go up
49. Ascertain- determine
50. Asceticism – one who leads a life of austerity for religious purposes
51. Aspersion- lie, detraction
52. Aspire- strive
53. Assail- reviles, assault, impugn, vilify
54. Assent- acquiescence, agreement, accede
55. Assiduous- diligent, sedulous, careful
56. Assignation- rendezvous
57. Asunder- to pieces, apart
58. Atelier- workshop, studio
59. Atone- beg pardon
60. Atrocious- horrible, iniquitous, inhuman
61. Audible- perceptible by the ear, discernable
62. Augury- clairvoyance, prognostication
63. Austere- harsh, grave, severe, acerbic
64. Autolatry – self worship
65. Avail- help
66. Avariciousness- avarice, greed
67. Averring- assert, depose, state
68. Averse- disinclined, repelled
69. Awe- wonder, fear, daunt

B

70. Balk- refuse, demur, frustrate
71. Barghest- dog shaped goblin
72. Basalt- dark glassy volcanic rock
73. Bastion- parapet, barbican
74. Batrachophagous – frog eater
75. Beclouding- obscure, darken
76. Bedlam- madhouse
77. Befuddle- confuses, muddle, inebriate
78. Behest- command, injunction
79. Belated- late
80. Bifurcated- furcated, split
81. Blanched- whitish
82. Blandishments- cajolery, gallantry, flattery
83. Blatant- obvious, obtrusive, boisterous
84. Bletcherous – poor or disgusting design
85. Bombilate – to hum or buzz
86. Borborygmus – movement of gas in the intestines
87. Brash- brazen, impudent, saucy, rude
88. Bravado- pretense, grandiosity, bombast
89. Brevirostrate – a short nose or beak
90. Brocade- needlework
91. Brontide – rumbling noise
92. Brood- offspring, sulk, incubate, meditate morbidly
93. Bullion- cast metal, ingot, slag, slug
94. Bulwark- wall, defense
95. Buoyant- floatable, cheerful
96. Buoyed- floating marker, beacon, signal
97. Burnished- glistening, coruscating, effulgent
98. Buttressed- prop, prop up, stanchion, bolster

C

99. Cabalistic- scheme, trick
100. Cachet- stamp, signet
101. Cachinnation – to laugh loud
102. Cacoethes – irresistible urge
103. Cadaverous- like a corpse, pallid, sallow
104. Cajole- coax
105. Calamity- adversity, tragedy
106. Callipygian – beautiful buttocks
107. Callous- hardened, inured, apathetic, obdurate
108. Capering- prank, frolic, fiasco
109. Capitulate- surrender
110. Capon- rooster
111. Capricious- fickle, heedless
112. Carnal- fleshly, sexual Carrion- decaying flesh
113. Castigate- rebuke
114. Casuistry- fallacious reasoning, fallacy
115. Cataclysmic- disastrous, violent
116. Cataleptic- unconscious, lethargic, torpid
117. Catechize- instruct, interrogate
118. Causeuse – upholstery built for two people
119. Cavalcade- parade
120. Cavil- censure, criticize
121. Certitude- confidence
122. Cessation- stopping
123. Chicane- trick, cozenage
124. Cicerone- doorman, escort
125. Circumambient- surrounding, enclosing
126. Circumspection- caution, prudence
127. Clamorous- noisy, vociferous
128. Clandestine- covert
129. Clarity- clearness, limpidity
130. Clemency- compassion, mildness, leniency
131. Cleptobiosis – stealing food
132. Cloying- luscious, sweet
133. Coalescing- united
134. Codicil- addendum, rider
135. Cogitate- ponder
136. Colossus- huge statue, of enormous size and importance
137. Comber- wave, roller, whitecap
138. Comeuppance- deserving
139. Commiserate- empathize, sorrow
140. Compel- force, bend, control
141. Complicity- machination, conspiracy, artifice, cabal, collusion, complot

142. Concupiscence- desire
143. Condemn- censure, find guilty, forbid
144. Conducive- favorable
145. Congeal- solidify, coagulate
146. Connotation- implied meaning, insinuate
147. Conspicuous- noticeable, eminent, flagrant
148. Contemplate- looks at, meditate, intend
149. Contention- contest, debate, claim
150. Contentious- argumentative
151. Contested- subject to controversy, polemical, contentious
152. Contrite- repentant, sorry
153. Contrition- penitence, sorrow, spite, compunction
154. Contumelies- arrogance
155. Convocation- gathering
156. Correspondence- being alike, accord, exchange of letters
157. Corsairs- buccaneer, filibuster, picaroon, pirate
158. Cortege- train, caravan
159. Cosmoses – orderly, harmonious
160. Countenance- Appearance, face, approval, aid
161. Covenant- agreement
162. Credulous- believing, green
163. Crimson- sanguine, bloody
164. Croupier- card games, banker, dealer, player
165. Cruciverbalist – loves crossword puzzles
166. Cupola- arched gateway
167. Cybernetic – theoretical study of control process of biological,
    mechanical and electronic systems
168. Cynosure- celebrity

D

169. Dactylonomy – counting using fingers
170. Dais- throne, cathedra
171. Dastardly- craven, nasty, timid
172. Debased- debauched, vitiated, perverted
173. Debauchery- orgies, revelry, desire
174. Declamatory- eloquent, elocutionary, pompous
175. Defenestrate – to throw something out a window
176. Deft- skilled, adroit, apt
177. Dehisce – to burst open
178. Delude- deceive, cozen
179. Demented- insane
180. Demure- prim, modest, coy
181. Denigrate- disparage, ridicule
182. Deposition- declaration, discharge
183. Depot- storehouse, storehouse, annex
184. Depredations- preying on, pillage
185. Derision- disdain, scorn, mockery
186. Descrying- find, ascertain
187. Desist- stop
188. Despatch- dispatch, news bulletin, haste, send, kill, finish
189. Despondent- depressed, forlorn
190. Despot- autocrat, tyrant
191. Diabolical- devilish, fiendish
192. Didactic- academic, pedagogical, preachy
193. Digamy – second marriage after the death of a spouse
194. Dilettante- amateur, connoisseur, aesthete
195. Dilute- watery, thin
196. Discern- notice, determine
197. Disconsolately- sad, gloomy
198. Discontent- dissatisfied
199. Disheveled- rumpled
200. Disposition- nature, predilection, management, endowment, grouping, settlement
201. Dissuade- persuade not to, daunt, thwart
202. Distrait- preoccupied
203. Dogma- doctrine, tenets
204. Dour- dismal
205. Draconian - very severe, exceedingly harsh
206. Draughty- atmospheric, airy
207. Dread- terrible, formidable, fear, dire, reverence
208. Dubious- doubtful, ambiguous, moot
209. Durance- term, interval

E

210. Ebullient- enthusiastic
211. Ecumenical- wholeness, totality
212. Edify- educate, teach, enlighten
213. Effrontery- brashness, insolence, audacity
214. Effusive- talkative, expansive
215. Eloquent- articulate, mellifluous
216. Emaciated- gaunt
217. Eminent- distinguished, high
218. Emissary- agent, proxy, delegate
219. Emphatic- definite, important
220. Encomiums- praise, panegyric
221. Enmity- animosity, rancor
222. Ennui- weary
223. Ensorcelled- under a magic spell, hexed
224. Entail- make necessary, evoke
225. Enthrall- fascinate, bewitch
226. Enthuse- elevate, rhapsody
227. Ephemeral- ephemeron, corposant, fleeting
228. Epicurean- fond of sensuous pleasure, gourmet
229. Epistle- letter
230. Epitaph- inscription, eulogy, elegy
231. Epithet- name, appellation, caption, tittle
232. Epitome- abstract, archetype
233. Equivocal- equivalence
234. Eradicate- obliterate
235. Erect- vertical, build, establish, set-up
236. Errant- aberrant, erratic
237. Erratic- eccentric, irregular
238. Erroneous- inaccurate
239. Erudition- learnedness
240. Espionage- spying
241. Espouse – adoption of or support for a cause or idea
242. Estrapade – A horse trying to kick off a rider
243. Etiquette- code of behavior, amenities
244. Evanescent- ephemeral, transient, brief
245. Evince- makes clear
246. Excoriate- denounce harshly
247. Exculpatory- tending to prove guiltless
248. Exhilarate- invigorate
249. Exhort- advise strongly, entreat
250. Exhume- disinter, unearth, resurrect
251. Exigencies- urgency
252. Expiate- atone, absolve, forgive
253. Exploit- accomplishment, take advantage of

254. Exquisite- beautiful, ethereal, acute, choice, refined
255. Extenuating- make less serious, palliate
256. Extirpate- annihilate
257. Extricate- clear away, extract
258. Exultant- elevate, glorify, please

F

259. Facet- aspect
260. Facile- easy, skilled, glib
261. Farce- absurd situation, exaggerated comedy
262. Farctate – filled, not hollow
263. Fatuous- dim-witted
264. Fealty- obligation of loyalty owed by a vassal, faithfulness
265. Feeble- ineffective, feckless, frail, dim
266. Fetes- feast, repast
267. Fetid- stinking, malodorous, putrid
268. Fiat – an arbitrary order or decree, let it be done
269. Fidelity- faithfulness, accuracy
270. Filial- dutiful, obedient
271. Filigree- lacework, tracery
272. Filipendulous – hanging by a thread
273. Flayed- denounce harshly, excoriate, disparage
274. Florid- excessively ornate, gaudy
275. Flout- scoff at
276. Frivolous- trivial, paltry, silly
277. Feudal – land granting in exchange for homage or military
     protection of Medieval Times
278. Fugue- overture, toccata
279. Fulminate- explode, shout at
280. Fusillade- simultaneous firing, salvo cannonade
281. Futile- vain, trivial

G

282. Gale- storm
283. Galvanized- animated, roused
284. Garrulities- talkative, verbose
285. Gauche- clumsy, maladroit, tactless
286. Genial- friendly, mild
287. Genuflected- get down on one's knees
288. Gibbet- execute, hang, lynch
289. Gimlet- awl, bit
290. Gingham- yarn dyed cotton fabric, stripes, plaids, solids
291. Golgotha- hill of Calvary where Jesus was crucified
292. Gourd- long-handled utensil, ladle
293. Graft- insert a shoot, fraud
294. Grandeur- magnificence, opulence
295. Gravity- heaviness, importance
296. Grotesque- hideous, ridiculous
297. Gunwales- upper edge of ship side
298. Gyroscope - powered engine compass of free-floating origin.

H

299. Habardasher- dealer in men's furnishings
300. Hamlet- village
301. Harangue- speech, tirade, address, bombast
302. Harebell- plant, Bluebell
303. Harridan- witch
304. Harrier- hawk or hound that hunts
305. Haunt- appear as a phantom, place often visited, trouble the mind, frequent
306. Hegemony- ascendancy, dominion
307. Hegira- precipitate flight, exodus
308. Heinous- atrocious, nefarious
309. Heresy- dissenting view, apostasy
310. Hitherto- previously
311. Hortatory- farming, rustic
312. Hue- color, cast, value
313. Hyssop- hyssop

I

314. Ignobly- inferior, lowborn
315. Imbue – to permeate or invade
316. Immure- enclose, corral
317. Impanel- to enroll (a jury)
318. Impetus – impulse or stimulus
319. Impeach- accuse of misconduct in office, inculpate
320. Impecunious- poor
321. Imperative- essential, domineering
322. Imperious- domineering, mandatory
323. Impertinence- insolence
324. Impetuous- impulsive
325. Importunate- urge persistently
326. Impudence- insolence, flippancy
327. Impunity- exemption, privilege
328. Inadvertent- unintentional, negligent
329. Incandescent- glowing from heat, effulgent
330. Inaniloquent – speaking foolishly
331. Incendiary- political agitator, iconoclast
332. Incensed- angry, indignant
333. Incongruous- inappropriate, inconsonant, inconsistent, strange
334. Inconspicuous- hardly noticeable, unobtrusive, obscure
335. Incumbent- in office, obligatory
336. Indemnify- pays off
337. Indignation- consternation, ire, fury, wrath
338. Ineradicable- permanent, ineffaceable, indelible
339. Inexorable- relentless
340. Inexorably- indispensably, vitally
341. Infamous- disreputable, wicked
342. Infatuation- crush, obsession
343. Inferno- phlogiston, blaze, pyre
344. Infidel- atheist, cynic
345. Ingratiate- persuade, seduce
346. Inimical- adverse, hostile
347. Iniquity- evil
348. Innate- inborn, connate
349. Innuendo- sly remark, allusion, aspersion, imputation, aside
350. Inoculate- give a shot
351. Inquest- judicial inquiry
352. Inquisitors- one who analyzes
353. Inscrutable- unfathomable, vexing
354. Insidious- guileful, evil, sly
355. Insinuate- intimate, instill
356. Integral- complete, essential
357. Intent- firm, purpose, meaning

358. Interpolated- interject
359. Interrogative- question, query
360. Invective- abusive, scurrilous
361. Inviolate- intact, pure
362. Involute- intricate, complex
363. Irascibly- irritable, choleric, petulant
364. Iridescent- shimmering, prismatic
365. Irk- bother, vex
366. Irrefragable- indisputable

J-L

J

367. Jaunty- dashing, rakish
368. Jesuit- of the roman church, ultramontane, papal
369. Jibe- Change sail, harmonize, be in accord, gibe, taunt
370. Jocular- witty, jocose, facetious, comic
371. Joust- tilt, tourney, match, duel
372. Jumentous – strong smell (like urine)

K

373. Kaleidoscopic- motley, colorful, complex

L

374. Lacuna- respite, hiatus, break
375. Laden- loaded
376. Lalochezia – relief using vulgar language
377. Languid- lackadaisical, weary
378. Languish- fail, long for
379. Largess- donation
380. Lattice- bower, grotto, arbor, gazebo, pergola
381. Laudable- commendable, exemplary
382. Layette- layette
383. Laggards – straggler
384. Lethargy- sluggishness
385. Lethologica – inability to recall something
386. Leviathan- huge sea mammal, beluga
387. Levity- lightness
388. Liaison- means of communication
389. Licentious- immoral, sensual, abandoned
390. Litany- religious song
391. Litigation- lawsuit
392. Livid- discoloration of skin, pallid with rage, angry
393. Loiter- linger, tarry
394. Lucid- bright, clear, sane
395. Ludicrous- laughable, farcical
396. Luminary- notable, sage

M

397. Macabre- horrible, weird
398. Macerate- moistens, soften, intenerate, sodden
399. Maladroit- awkward, tactless
400. Maledicent – speaking slanderous or abusive
401. Malevolence- hatred
402. Malfeasance- impropriety, mischief
403. Malice- hostility, malevolence
404. Maligned- malevolent, pernicious, baleful, evil, accuse
405. Mammothrept – A child raised and spoiled by his or her grandmother
406. Manacle- handcuffs, shackles, fetters
407. Mandate- command, fiat, injunction
408. Manifest- apparent, display, prove
409. Manifold – having many features or forms
   Maundering- inarticulate
410. Melancholy- sad, pensive
411. Mellow- genial, melodious, ripe, softened, mature
412. Meretricious- gaudy, tawdry
413. Meticulous- careful, fastidious, finical, exact
414. Miasma- swamp exhalations, effluvium, gas
415. Milieu – environment or setting
416. Misogynist – a person who hates or mistreats women
417. Missive- letter, epistle, note
418. Mitigate- relieves, allay, mollify
419. Mnemonic- mnemonic
420. Modicum – small or token amount
421. Monastic – secluded and contemplative, monastery or con
422. Monolith – a large organization that acts as a powerful unit vent
423. Moot- controversial
424. Mulct- defraud, fleece, fine
425. Mulligrubs – ill temper, grumpy
426. Mumpsimus – a person who persists in mistaken practices
427. Munificent- generous
428. Muslin- sturdy plain weave cotton fabric
429. Myopia- astigmatic, nearsighted

N

430. Nave- central part of church, hub of wheel
431. Nebulous- indistinct, hazy, cloudy
432. Nemesis- destiny, kismet, karma, doom
433. Nirvana- paradise, Elysium, Arcadia
434. Nondescript- uninteresting, amorphous
435. Notoriety- fame, repute
436. Null- invalid, nothing, unreal, worthless

O

437. Obdurate- unyielding, shameless
438. Obeisance- homage, bow, honor
439. Oblate- drink, sacrifice, gift
440. Obloquy- disgrace, defamation, blame
441. Obsequiously- submissive, groveling
442. Obtrude- get in on, meddle
443. Obviated- prevent
444. Offal- trash
445. Ominous- doomed, inauspicious, dismal
446. Omnivore- avid, rapacious, greedy
447. Onerous- heavy, tiresome
448. Onychophagy – nail biting habit
449. Orator- shrewd person
450. Ordination- investiture, coronation, induction

P

451. Pagan- pagan
452. Palanquin- east Asian covered and carried litter
453. Pall- gloom, coffin cover, satiate
454. Palsied- shaking
455. Pandiculation - stretching
456. Parapet- wall, palisade
457. Parasol- umbrella, parapluie
458. Pariah- social outcast
459. Parlance- speech
460. Pathos- poignancy, emotion
461. Peculiar- unusual, characteristic
462. Pecuniary – relating to money, wealth
463. Pedantic- academic, didactic
464. Penurous- indigence
465. Perdition- destruction, doom, hell
466. Perfidious- dishonest, mean, treacherous
467. Perfunctorily- indifferent, heedless, slovenly
468. Pergola- arbor, kiosk
469. Perilous- dangerous, precarious
470. Peripatetic- travelling on foot, of Aristotle philosophy
471. Perjury- willful lie, violation of oath
472. Perspicacity- insight
473. Perturbation- disturbance, consternation
474. Pester- annoy, harry, hector
475. Pestilent- lethal
476. Pettifogging- shyster, trickster
477. Petulant- irritable, cross
478. Phalanx- army
479. Phantom- apparition, hallucinatory, specter
480. Philanthropist- humanitarian
481. Piecemeal- piece by piece
482. Pinnacle- apex, acme, zenith
483. Piquant- spicy, stimulating, racy
484. Placards- poster, manifesto, post
485. Placate- appease, conciliate
486. Placid- peaceful, tranquil, serene
487. Platitude- cliché, inanity, bromide, triteness
488. Plausible- specious, deceptive, convincing
489. Plea- appeal, supplication, imploration, defense
490. Plenary- full, whole, absolute
491. Pliable- flexible, tractable
492. Poised- balance, composure, bearing
493. Posse (comitatus)- group of men to aid peace
494. Postulate – to assume or assert the truth or reality

495. Prerogative- right
496. Prescience- foreknowledge
497. Preside- direct, officiate
498. Prestidigitation- legerdemain, slight-of-hand
499. Pretense- dishonesty, disguise
500. Preternatural- irregular, peculiar
501. Proclivity- inclination, bias
502. Proffered- offer, tender, suggest
503. Profligate- dissolute, dissolute, depraved, salacious
504. Prognosticate- forecast
505. Promulgated- proclaim
506. Propitious- auspicious, favorably inclined
507. Proprietor- owner, heritor
508. Prorogue- postpone
509. Prosecute- file suit, litigate
510. Proselytize- persuade, brainwash
511. Prostrate- supine, exhausted, overcome, overthrown, abase, differential
512. Pugnacious- belligerent, irascible, truculent
513. Puritan- flagellant, penitent
514. Pyknic – a fat or rounded body

Q-R

Q

515. Quagmire- swamp, fen, slough, difficulty
516. Querulous- petulant, caviling, complaining
517. Quidnunc – gossiper
518. Quiescent- quiet, serene, placid, still

R

519. Ramparts- barrier
520. Rapacious- greedy
521. Rapier- fencing sword
522. Rapt- engrossed, intent, enchanted
523. Realm- domain, sovereignty
524. Rebuke- disapproval, remonstration, reprimand
525. Rebus- puzzle, conundrum
526. Recalcitrant- rebellious, contumacious
527. Recipient- person receiving, legatee
528. Recompense- payment, amends, indemnification
529. Redolent- fragrant
530. Redound- have an effect, return, recoil, accrue, contribute
531. Remit- send, pardon, relay, postpone
532. Reprobate- depraved, miscreant
533. Repudiate- reject
534. Repudiation- renunciation, denial
535. Requite- compensate, retaliate
536. Rescission- revocation
537. Resounding- reverberating
538. Respite- rest, suspension, delay
539. Retaliate- requites, repay, avenge
540. Reticence- taciturnity, reserve, shyness
541. Retire- withdraws, regress, abdicate
542. Rhetoric- eloquence, pomposity
543. Rheumy- water discharge from the nose or eyes
544. Ribald- lascivious, indecent, lewd, salacious
545. Ricochet- rebound
546. Rivulet- inlet, estuary
547. Ruminate- ponder, muse
548. Runcation – weeding out
549. Rusty- color, oxidation, corrode

S

550. Sagely- sagacious, judicious, prudent, philosopher
551. Salient- important, prominent
552. Sallow- pale, ashen
553. Salubrious- healthful, sanitary
554. Salve- emollient, cerate, unction
555. Sanctify- bless
556. Sanctuary- church, adytum, chancel, retreat
557. Sardonic- sarcastic, mordent, wry, morbid
558. Savage- uncultivated, angry, inhuman, animal
559. Savory- delicious
560. Scarlet- vermilion, color, red
561. Schism- split, cabal
562. Scion- descendant, shoot, branch
563. Scoundrel- scoundrel, imp
564. Sculled- boat, raft
565. Sectarian- dissenter, zealot, rebel
566. Secular – worldly rather than spiritual
567. Senescence- decrepitude, dotage, senility
568. Shoal- sandbank
569. Shrewd- sharp, sly
570. Sibilance- sound, fricative
571. Slated- ballot
572. Smelt – to melt or fuse (ores) to separate metallic constituents
573. Sobriety- abstinence, solemnity
574. Solace- comfort, console, relieve
575. Solemn- grave, grand, pensive
576. Solicit- supplicate, stimulate, ask, seduce, peddle
577. Somber- dark, gloomy, dusky
578. Sonorous- resonant, loud
579. Soporific- sleepy
580. Sorties- foray, sally, attack
581. Sovereign – paramount, supreme, excellent, head of state of a
    monarchy
582. Sotto voce- out of range
583. Spry- agile, nimble
584. Spurious- false
585. Staccatically- crisp, sharp, abrupt
586. Stalwart- strong, braves, robust, resolute
587. Statutory- authorized
588. Staunch- constant, loyal
589. Stevedores- dock worker, deck-hand, laborer
590. Stigmatic- disgrace, besmirch
591. Strife- conflict
592. Suavely- sophisticated, urbane

593. Subdue- defeat, tame, soften
594. Subterfuge- device, ploy, deceit
595. Succor- help
596. Suety- fatty, oily, soapy
597. Sufficient- adequate, sufficing
598. Superfluous- excessive, exorbitant, profuse
599. Superlative- superior to all others, unrivalled, utmost
600. Supplicant- mendicant, suppliant, beggar, cadger, almsman
601. Suppurated- discharge pus, decay
602. Surreptitious- secret, clandestine
603. Suzerainty- regime, incumbency
604. Sward- dirt with grass
605. Sybarite- sensualist, hedonist, voluptuary, Epicurean
606. Sycophant- fawner
607. Syncopated- abbreviate, epitomized

T

608. Tachyphagia – eating rapid or fast
609. Taciturn- reticent, silent
610. Tarantism – uncontrollable impulse to dance
611. Tatterdemelies- person wearing tattered clothes, ragamuffin
612. Taunt- insult, ridicule
613. Taut- tense
614. Tedious- tiresome
615. Temerity- audacity
616. Tensile- ductile, capable of being stretched
617. Tenuous- slender, insubstantial
618. Tepid- lukewarm, indifferent
619. Tergiversation- desertion, apostasy, withdrawal
620. Throng- crowd, multitude. Horde
621. Tier- line, array, bank
622. Timorous- fearful
623. Tithe- one tenth of income taxed for government or church
624. Titillate- excite, arouse
625. Tonsure- use a razor
626. Tourney- tournament
627. Transverse- cross, oblique, thwart
628. Treacherous- traitorous, perfidious, unreliable
629. Trebled- three-way
630. Tremulous- timid, afraid, shaking
631. Trinity – a group of three closely related members
632. Trousseau- special wardrobe that a bride assembles for her marriage
633. Truculent- fierce, mean, cruel
634. Truncated- deformed
635. Tumult- disturbance, excitement
636. Turbulent- agitated

U-Z

U

637. Ubiquitous – omnipresent – to be or seem to be everywhere at once
638. Ulotrichous – wooly or crispy hair
639. Unanimous- agreed, unified
640. Unctuousness- undue compliments, sycophancy
641. Unduly- extremely
642. Unprepossessing- unattractive
643. Untenable- unreasonable
644. Urbane- suave, cosmopolitan
645. Urbane- suave, elegant
646. Usufructuary – having use of property
647. Usurer- extortionist, vampire
648. Usurp- seize, expropriate

V

649. Vacillate- waver, sway
650. Vacuity- emptiness
651. Vain- useless, otiose, egotistical
652. Vassal- serf, chattel, thrall, servant, slave
653. Vigesimation – the act of killing every 20th person
654. Vehemently- fervent, zealous, ardent
655. Venal- corrupt
656. Venal- corrupt, sordid, bribable
657. Venerable- esteemed, ancient
658. Venire- writ ordered by a judge to summon jurors
659. Venue- locality of where a crime is committed
660. Veranda- terrace, piazza
661. Verbose- loquacious, wordy, pleonastic, prolix
662. Verities- truth, verisimilitude
663. Vermin- arthropod, creepy crawler
664. Venery- pursuit, hunt
665. Vestments- clothes, raiment
666. Vicinity- neighborhood, milieu
667. Vicissitudes- unpredictable changes
668. Vigorous- powerful, dynamic, zealous
669. Vile- evil, nefarious, repulsive, obscene, contemptible, paltry
670. Violate- breach, transgress, rape
671. Viraginity – masculine qualities of women

672. Vitalize- animate, strengthen
673. Vitriol- animadversion, faultfinding
674. Vivacity- liveliness, vigor
675. Volatile- evaporating quickly, flighty, fleeting
676. Vouchsafed- award

W

677. Wan- pale, haggard
678. Wanton- careless, lewd, lavish,
679. Wayfarer- journeyer
680. Wistful- sad, longing
681. Woe- sorrow, agony
682. Wraith- ghost, shade
683. Writ- law, edict, document

X

684. Xerophagy – a Lenton fast

Y

Z

685. Zeal – enthusiastic devotion to a cause
686. Zealous- enthusiastic, fervid
687. Zenith- highest point, culminating point
688. Zest- relish, piquancy, taste